Chronicles from the East during the Great War

CHRONICLES FROM THE EAST DURING THE GREAT WAR

* * *

Sapper James P McIntosh
& Wendy J Grigor

Published in 2022 by Birchview Books

ISBN: 978-1-3999-3485-5

Publishing services by
www.lumphananpress.co.uk

© Wendy J Grigor 2022

Every effort has been made to trace relevant copyright holders

Printed and bound by Imprint Digital

Acknowledgements

I would like to thank my friend Kath for taking the time to help me with this book. Also, my daughter Laura for her encouragement to continue and for her support. After all these years I would like to think my grandfather would be proud that stories of his WW1 experiences, some of them humorous, have finally made it to print.

At the back of the book I have also included a short memorial to his elder son, Stanley. His other son Ronald joined the Merchant Navy Blue Star Line where he worked for many years, eventually rising to the rank of Chief Engineer and seeing many different countries.

– Wendy J Grigor

CONTENTS

Acknowledgements	5
Introduction	9
The Unexpected	14
Men I Met On My Army Career	22
Humour	35
The Bus Horse	40
Army Hospital	41
The Indian Navy	42
Uqbah	43
Furlough	47
Khan Baghdadi	65
Temperance	71
In The East Time Is Of No Account	72
The Call Of The East	73
Mosul	74
Babylon	76
Brief Historical Notes On Babylon	82
The Tower Of Babel	84
Code Of Khummurabi	87
Conclusion	89
Stanley McIntosh	90

Introduction

World War One began in the summer of 1914, after the assassination of Archduke Franz Ferdinand of the Austro-Hungarian Empire and his wife, and ended on November 11th, 1918. Over 700,000 British servicemen lost their lives during this time. It was known as The Great War and was fought simultaneously on several fronts involving many different nationalities. What you are about to read has come from notes that were made by my grandfather whilst he was on active service during the Mesopotamia campaign. His name was James Porter McIntosh. I dedicate this book to him and all those that were involved in World War One.

James Porter McIntosh was born in Aberdeen at 8 Innes Street on 17th August 1887. He was married on 23rd August 1913 and was blessed with a baby son. In 1916 he enlisted and went to train at three different army centres in England before moving to the draft depot. He sailed away from England on the evening of 8th October 1916, heading to Mesopotamia to strengthen troops already stationed there.

From his notes I was able to compile memoirs showing a small part of what life would have been like on the Mesopotamian front. After discharge from army service he returned to civilian life, home to his wife and baby son, and resumed his work. He enjoyed family life, completing his family with the birth of another son Ronald.

Sadly, in January 1963, family life was to be cruelly shattered with the death of his oldest son Stanley, who was killed in his line of work as assistant firemaster. You can read about this in the final chapter.

In his later life James retired from work as a Civil Servant after forty-five and a half years, where he received the Imperial Service Medal. He went on to live until 10th November 1967 and is buried at Allenvale Cemetery in Aberdeen. (His elder son Stanley is also interred at Allenvale Cemetery.)

Family photograph. Mr JP McIntosh, wife Mary, Stanley, at front Ronald.

Sapper James P McIntosh
Service Number 17208 Royal Engineers

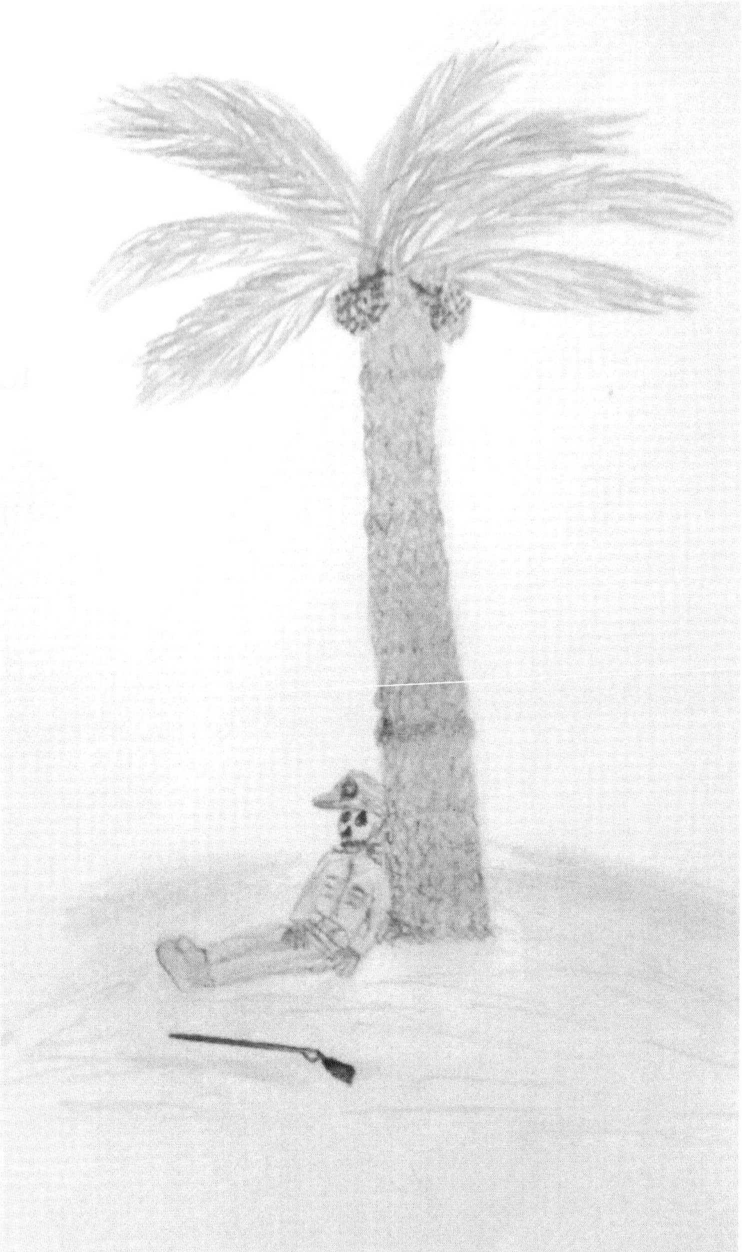

The story I am about to unfold,
In a very few words is easily told,
Tis of an R.E of the Sigs don't you see,
who came out to Mespot and got badly sold,

For King and country was all in his eye,
When he joined the R.Es as a poor humble Pi,
But the sun by degrees, reduced him to grease,
Now his last resting place in the desert does lie.

He was so overcome by the heat one day,
Unto himself he thus did say,
"I see a nice palm, it is my jam,
by its shadow I will from the sun keep away."

In the shade of the palm, he soon fell asleep
While the sun on its way a few points did creep
And in a small mound, his remains were found
Boots, rifle and uniform, with cap badge complete.

The Unexpected

It is the unexpected that happens. A year ago, little did I dream I would travel so far in my life, yet here I am in Mesopotamia.

After undergoing the usual training at three centres in England I duly found myself booked to do my little bit, but far from home. I was on draft for the furthest away front: Mesopotamia.

Leaving the draft depot on a Sunday evening, 8th October 1916, and travelling all night we duly found ourselves on board the transport and sailed that same evening.

Only when the shores of England had disappeared in the mist did I actually realise I was on "active service". Prior to this life had been very pleasant and many friendships I had established but as the shores of England receded gradually a realisation of what I was leaving behind took hold of me. For the first time I knew what it meant to part from all one holds sacred and dear.

Our ultimate destination we knew, but instead of going the short route owing to trouble in the Mediterranean, we were taken the long route around the Cape.

Of the voyage little can be said. Comfort there was none due to the overcrowding which was so great that I only slept below on two nights. As regards the feeding, now that it is past it remains but like a faded dream, and the least said the better. When I state that the maggots could be seen in the cooked rice you can form your own idea of the conditions. Providence, however, smiled on us as we had no serious case on board, no epidemic and no rough weather worth mentioning. Even when we crossed the Equator so cold was it that many were actually wearing their overcoats.

The only good thing I can say about our transport was that as a sea boat it was perfection, and a tribute to our navy for it was a prize captured from the Germans and refitted as a British Transporter.

On board our time was occupied reading, writing, attending lectures on various subjects, physical drill, roll calls and guard duties. General duties took the form of assistance to the lookout, owing to the submarine nuisance. Happy am I to state we never sighted one, the nearest approach to a periscope being an empty wooden soap box which floated harmlessly past our ship.

On the voyage we put in at three ports: Daker, W.A Durban and Bombay.

Daker is a beautiful port and as a town is deliciously laid out, having fine wide-open thoroughfares. Its harbour, being natural, should soon become the premier port of call on the west coast. Its coaling arrangements are of the latest and speediest type. Here we were taken for route marches during the four days occupied in coaling and watering.

It was very hot, so hot in fact that never before had I seen men sweat so much. There was hardly a soldier whose drill uniform was not saturated with sweat while the beads ran down their faces. Here we received a huge disappointment. We were taken on a bathing parade but when we reached the place decided on, sharks could be seen waiting for us, so naturally we declined the invitation to enter.

The welcome we received at Durban is a thing which none

of us on board that ship shall ever forget. From the moment we touched the wharf till we set sail we became practically the guests of the citizens of Durban. All the public institutions were thrown open to us free of charge and many of the citizens actually kidnapped our men, taking them to their homes to feed and entertain them. Then when they returned to the ship they were sent loaded with the good things of the earth.

Durban as a city is very up-to-date. Its streets are clean and well laid out and it has beautiful promenades along the sea front. Here there is open air as well as enclosed and mixed bathing. Electric cars run to all parts of the city and, being free from 3 pm to 11 pm, we got a thorough sight of the town. Tobacco was very cheap while other goods were dear, but the city seems full of prosperity.

The first place I went to was the swimming pond which is even better than our own at home, but the water tastes the same. This pond was in the centre of the city and two miles from the sea, so you see Durban is even further ahead than Aberdeen for it has uptown baths. The zoo at Durban is very good and quite equal to the London one. The exhibits are very fresh. Originally it was a private one but was handed over to the town and has thrived ever since and is still extending.

It was intended to hold our ship's sports at Durban as we expected to be there three days, but alas it was not to be as orders were received to sail the next day. We left England practically "Unhonoured and Unsung" for we stole away quietly without any flare or trumpets and only the Godspeed of a few in the know, but what we lost in this respect in England was made up for by the Durbanists. Scotsman and Aberdonian as I am, never have I been so moved as with the lavish hospitality given by Durban.

Crowds cheered us and waved farewells until we were out

of sight. We lay off Bombay for a week and were taken off the ship in lighters, fore one day, aft the next, for route marches.

Bombay was very interesting. It is full of that glamour which the east alone can cast. While ashore I always seemed to be in a trance. What with the various types of natives and their different and many coloured dresses fluttering about so silently, carts drawn by bullocks, and the heat of the sun, I really felt as if I had dropped from another world. Even for the short time I was ashore I felt that in India here was a land of unfathomable mysteries and greatness.

Leaving Bombay and after a six-day sail we were transferred at sea to another ship drawing less water. In the ship we finished our eight-week voyage. If we had grumbled aboard our first ship, we had good cause to grumble on our second, and it was a mercy we were there only one night and a day.

So great was the vermin on board that few made any attempt to sleep. The cockroaches were numberless and the rats were so numerous that one crowd spent the night catching them, the method they employed being the same as rabbit poachers who use the string with the loop.

The trip up the Shatel Arab was very enjoyable. Date palm trees grow close to each bank, and their green colour was pleasing to the eyes after seeing nothing but the expanse of the ocean.

On the way up we passed the two ships sunk in the river by the Turks to block it. The river craft were a source of great interest to us. In due course we were transferred to a lighter and duly landed at our base.

Our first day in Mesopotamia was a revelation. We were led to believe so difficult was the transportation of goods that bully beef and biscuits would be our daily fare. Judge our joy when we discovered fresh bread and meat served daily. So well are things organised out here that we even receive forty cigarettes or tobacco in lieu and two boxes of matches per week. Not only in transport have things reached a high level but also in developing the country. As an illustration one fellow who had been up the line some months on returning to the base didn't recognise the place.

When he left only the tents had been pitched and when he returned good serviceable roads had been built, huts electrically lighted erected, with the place being even like a model city. The only drawback here is the great scarcity of water. All water for drinking and cooking purposes has to be chemically treated and often has to be carried miles.

Mesopotamia is teeming full of historical and religious interest. What is claimed as the site of the Garden of Eden is that tract of land stretching northward where the Euphrates and Tigris meet to the ruins of ancient and mighty Babylon, the seat of the Chaldean Empire. Here reigned the great Nebuchadnezzar in the proudest and grandest city of his time. His name recalls the captivity of the Children of Israel, Daniel in the Lion's Den, the fiery furnace and the episode of the writing on the wall foretelling the doom of Nebuchadnezzar's mighty city whose ruins can be seen today. Here also lie the remains of ancient Nineveh, that capital of the great Assyria, where Jonah was proceeding when, as the tale has it, he was swallowed by the whale. The domed tomb of the prophet Ezra still stands set in a clump of date palms on the left bank of the Tigris just below Amara.

By the same waters the exiled captives from the Jewish hill country across the desert to the west "sat down and wept". Their descendants are here to this day. There can be little doubt that this land was the cradle of the human race, here our rude forefathers awoke to the consciousness of purposeful activity, and they reaped the fruits of this rich alluvial plain.

Over this ground has been fought the greatest and most decisive battles in the world's history. Petty prince quarrels of the early days of civilization have been settled here and it has witnessed the mighty charges of Assyrian chariots and the massed formation of the Persian hordes. Cities which have been besieged and defended, pillaged and plundered by rival and adjacent states, or by wild barbarians from the steppes of Asia, today are relics of a few stones set in a desert waste.

Mesopotamia of today is practically a huge desert except on the banks of the two rivers where the date palm flourishes. The bulk of the inhabitants consist of nomad Bedouins or sedentary Arabs, the descendants of old Persian and Assyrian stocks, and Jews whose ancestors did not return to Palestine. The religion of the inhabitants is chiefly Muhammadanism, and little progress seems to have been made since Biblical times. The people dress just as they did then and little cultivation is done. Ploughing can still be seen as described in Scripture; the same plough drawn by oxen being still in use. The country was, up till the time of our landing, in the hands of the Turkish successors to the caliphate of Baghdad who have had possession for some three hundred years. At present the land is particularly desert due to the Turkish method of misgovernment and oppression, which has never made it worthwhile to spend labour or money in developing the land. The rivers abound in fish, turtles are plentiful, and lizards abound in many varieties. Other wild animal life is not plentiful. The lion which must have roamed during David's captivity is extinct and the only wild animal seen now, if it can so be classed, is the jackal. The jackal roams principally by night when it feeds on refuse and travels in flocks usually led by a hyena. The hyena acts as a guide having a strong sense of smell. The jackal is a cross between a dog and a fox. It has a fox's head, a dog's body and a tail like a wolf.

Wild birds are few, being chiefly carrion, crow, sparrow, hawks, wild duck and kingfishers. There is also a species of bird similar to our bullfinch known to the Indians as the bully-bully.

Although at present practically a desert, the ground is capable of cultivation. In days of old this was the granary of the world and with modern science, irrigation and railways there is no reason why it should not again blossom like the rose. Being central to three great continents it could easily become one of the richest grain producing countries in the world. This may be the result of our present efforts and sacrifice. The climate during the coldest period is similar to that of an Egyptian winter but the summers are extremely hot, 123 degrees in the shade being common. This, however, would be modified greatly by cultivation.

Meantime, flies are a pest to the country. The ordinary British house fly is so numerous I have counted no less than three hundred and fifty on a Strand Magazine page; as each fly multiplies by ten in the hot season an idea can be formed of the pest they are. The sand fly is the most dangerous to mankind as he carries disease but now our scientists are on his track, his death knell will soon be sounded.

A few of the present largest towns are:

Busra – situated fifty-seven miles from the sea on the right bank of the Shattel-Arab, population about 60,000 composed of Sedentary Arabs, Europeans, Indians, 5,000 Persians and 1,000 Jews.

Nasiriyah – a comparatively modern town 115 miles from Busra. Population 10,000. Stands on the left bank of the Euphrates.

Kut-el Amara – on the Tigris. A centre of grain traffic, population 4,000.

Amara – population 10,000 and 31 miles North of Qurnah on the Tigris caravan routes, between Kut and the Persian passes.

Baghdad – the largest city of Eastern Turkey in Asia, population about 140,000, of whom some 55,000 are Jews.

On the Tigris, about twenty-four miles from the nearest point on the Euphrates, prior to the war there was a large European colony. It was chiefly British and had a fine hospital, schools, a Jewish High school and a branch of the Church missionary society. It is about 500 hundred miles from Busra by the river route.

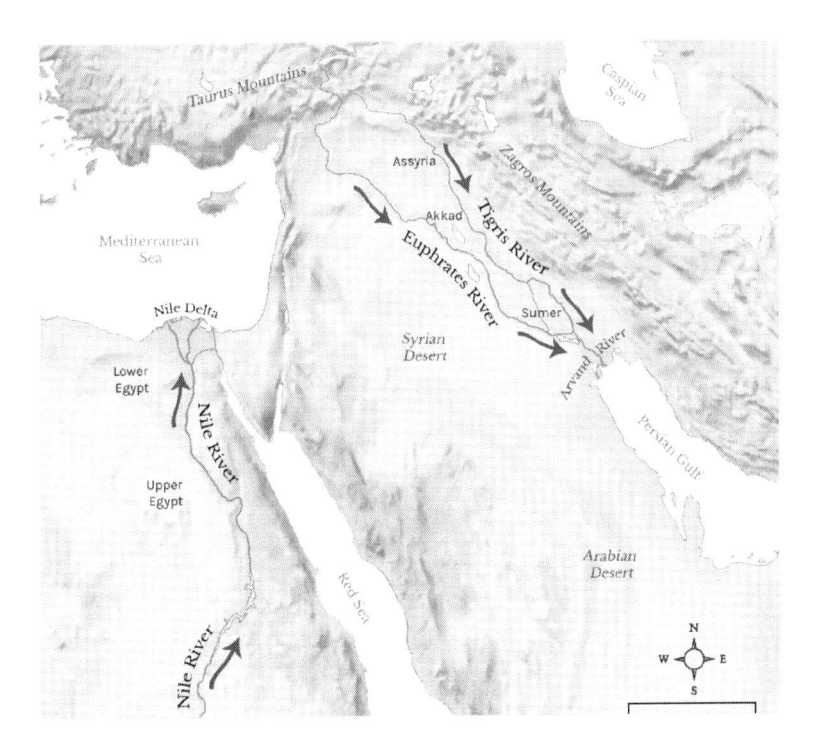

Men I Met On My Army Career

He was called Jack Young. Young may have been his name but young he was not, for his hair was iron grey while what moustache he had left was of the tartan variety – that is red well mixed with white. Jack was certainly a square peg in a round hole; this will be amply demonstrated when it is told that prior to becoming a member of the signal services he was to trade a Butcher.

The only recollection Jack had of his enlistment is the fact that he was accosted by the recruiting Sergeant who asked him if he knew anything about signalling, to which Jack replied that he did not. Before he awakened from his boozing spell he was enrolled in HM Forces.

It is with a twinkle of humour that Jack recounts not telling the Sergeant that the only signalling he knew was how to get the cows to the slaughterhouse, for his occupation was a killer.

Glasgow was his native City; there he was bred and born, and, in his estimation, the said city was the hub of the universe. Patriotism is a laudable thing but Jack overdid it, Scotland he held to the finest country in the world and nothing produced outside of it was of any value. Jack, to tell the truth, was but a poor specimen of a Scotsman and although told time and time again by brither Scots little effect had it on him.

By his own confession he lived a rather sodden life before the war. Payday saw most of his hard-earned cash within the coffers of his favourite pub. If ever an illustration of the good effects of Temperance were required Jack would have supplied it, for on the outward trip as no intoxicants were to be had Jack became a different looking man everyday. By the time we reached the front he looked as if we had renewed his youth.

The only good quality about Jack was the fact that he was always singing the praises of his wife. She was a beauty, and a grand housekeeper, and what not, in fact according to Jack, she was perfect.

Those of us who knew Jack's low habits sympathised with his wife he praised so. Yet it is strange that often a good woman will be found tied for life with a mate far inferior and many a man with a wife who drags him down.

Having little education, although a beautiful pen writer, Jack was always in trouble. One of his peculiarities when telling you anything was to leer into your face and point his finger at you, with the opening remark "I'se saying". Doing this once to a Depot Sergeant Major, Jack was duly rewarded with CB for five days for undue familiarity.

Jack portrayed little or no respect for religion of any description; he suited his belief to that of the person he was most likely to benefit by at the time being. A typical Glaswegian: when found useless to the service he came out for, he managed to drop into a nice canny job in the lines and there we will leave him for the present.

DICKIE PLAISTOW

My first acquaintance of Dick was made at the depot. He had just finished a 24-hour spell of duty and found ourselves down for another 12 without a break.

Dick took it so cheerfully, and his cheerfulness was such a contrast to the usual "grouse" that, as the story-tellers say, my heart warmed to him. From that time we became very friendly. Dick was medium height, smart in appearance, and when in doubt or perplexed by anything had a habit of shrugging his shoulders very like a Frenchman. This habit was probably hereditary for not only had he spent a good part of time in "La Belle France" but I have a recollection that he once told me he had descended from a French family.

Dick was a "homer". By homer, I mean one whose whole heart and soul is given to the welfare of his home and loved ones. At his duty he was very conscientious but had no desire for promotion. What he desired most was for everybody to do their utmost and so finish the war quickly and allow us to return the sooner. He was ably qualified for promotion having been well up in a Volunteer Corps but in his own words, "Let those who mean to make the army their career get promotions, I will be out of it as soon as the war is over."

Dick was very religious in the true Christian sense, but never paraded his beliefs. He practised what he believed in with a beautiful simplicity. Politically he was far seeing and could foretell how events would shape with a certainty which I thought uncanny. Dick used to complain and recognized he was not musical and always found himself at a disadvantage in company. This, however, was a libel on himself as he was an expert card trickster and conjurer, in fact so good was he I have seen many a worse professional. Bashfulness was one of his weakest points for he never presumed on anyone but once the ice of formality was broken a truer and more entertaining fellow would be hard to meet. Dick possessed a face which I term a mirror, for every emotion he passed through flashed across his countenance. In civil life Dick assisted his father in business, one that has stood the test of time. When Dick is on its history one fancies it is a recital from Dickens. To this and his wife and kiddies he will return. Roll on that time.

HG WILLIAMSON

"HG" as he was known to his inmates, Harry was one of these persons who to look at made one laugh. On close inspection I could never detect what was the cause for he was quite normal, but at first sight there was a peculiarity about him which moved one's humorous instinct. My first recollection of Harry was when he enlisted and had on his civilian clothes just before we received an army fit. When I contrast Harry of today with Harry as he was then it is truly a revelation of the army's ability to smarten up a man. When Harry came up to join, he looked exactly as if he had stepped out of the old curiosity shop. He wore large spectacles and a bowler hat and so odd was his appearance that it became generally understood he was a professor.

To see Harry today, so neat, trim and smart and youthful looking, it makes me wonder if my first impression of him was correct. Harry was always springing surprises on us. First we discovered he was an expert draught player, then in turn a singer and pianist and when a tiny whistle was produced Harry became a hot favourite, for he could coax any tune from it in beautiful mellow notes.

Harry's greatest failing was his stomach, and it was a standing joke that if he was wanted and couldn't be found he could always be run to earth at the YMCA canteen, or failing that the cook house.

Harry used to draw beautiful pictures of what his wife could cook and he enjoyed cooking at his watch, and then telling you what he would be having if he was at home. He possessed a very timid nature and was a little deaf but never did anyone an ill turn. He was always thinking of his home and kiddies. He was a first-rate artist and has drawn many a good picture. Taken all over he was a decent sort if rather fine for a soldier, though the life agreed with him.

BROWN

Brown was the limit. Everything he did was a failure. If he started to clean a rifle some part broke, even a bicycle the same. If he was asked to fetch anything or pass it along it always dropped when it reached Brown. Of him it was said a look would turn a thing wrong; a strange lad born of English parents in India, both he and his brother were enlisted young in the army. The brother differs from our Brown as black from white. The best said about Brown is that he is soft.

Having been brought up in India he was a bad partner for outpost. If the other chap is English, Brown can live like an Indian and on Indian food besides speak their language, which of course their language is a disadvantage for an Englishman.

FRANK

Frankie was the youngster of our crowd although he had seen 26 summers. He was the joy of our crowd too… he was ever smiling, a temperament I often envied. It is sunny natures like Frank's that makes soldiering enjoyable for when in awkward places a look of Frankie's smile dispelled the dark clouds. It has always been a mystery to me how Frankie managed to keep up the smile, for I know he worried a good deal about his wife and two kiddies, yet he never showed it but to a few.

A good footballer he carried his code of honour into ordinary life, and I never knew him do one underhand thing. As a storyteller he was a failure for many a yarn began by him has remained unfinished due to the fact that long er he was half done he couldn't proceed for laughing, and of course neither could we listen for laughing with him. Many a night he has entertained us with stories of Glasgow life which have never been recorded but which were true and therefore better than fiction which has been printed. Of a happy and healthy disposition, I hope the Gods of fortune will grant his return to his native town. Men such as he will be at a premium after this devastating war.

FREDDY

In the section he was always called Freddy although his real name was Stanley Anderson Armstrong. His father, a Major in the Indian army, gave his life to his king and country in the African war, thus leaving his two children orphans, his wife having died two years before her husband. Coming from soldier stock it was only natural that Freddy should follow in his father's footsteps and so the Great War found him prepared and although only 20 years old had held the post of mounted despatch rider for our section. He was a soldier of the true type. Everything he did was done for the Honour of the regiment and few could equal him in horsemanship.

Before coming out to the front Freddy had fallen madly in love with a young lady in India and on mail days poor Fred used to get terrible chaffed about the girl. Everybody would enquire how Mabel was, when he was to be married, if she sent her love and so on and so on.

The weary war dragged on and then to his great joy Fred was granted a furlough; it was a happy lad who set out for India.

Naturally his furlough was to be spent with Mabel who was up in a hill station, it being the hot season. After many hours of travel Freddy duly arrived at Mabel's residence but alas the course of true love never did run smooth, and our Fred found he was not wanted. During his absence a Lieutenant had been courting Mabel. As he was rich, her father had given her to this Lieutenant with his blessing, poor Fred never being thought about. Although Fred discovered Mabel still loved him he had perforce to return a very disappointed lad.

Fate plays some funny tricks and judge our surprise when our officer went sick, his place taken by none other than Fred's rival. It came about that in one engagement this rival of Fred's was entirely cut off from everybody and it so happened that Fred, after a struggle with his conscience, by his superb horsemanship rode out and amidst a hail of bullets brought the wounded lieutenant back to safety. It's an ill wind that blows nobody good. Freddy was duly given the VC and the lieutenant was so glad to escape being a dead man he settled a large sum on Fred. Further, when he discovered how things stood with Mabel and his rescuer, he waved his claim and insisted on Fred and her being married. The deed was duly carried out. The section pledged their health in a special ration of Johnnie Walker supplied by the officer who let us hope that the couple would live happy ever after.

GUS

As Gus he was known as a child and as Gus he will remain to all who have contact with him. His surname I will not mention lest my small pamphlet may come under his eye and the romantic touch I have built around him may be blown to pieces.

Being a bachelor standing six feet in his stockings and weighing over 15 stone he was certainly what could be truthfully called a man of weight.

In civilian life Gus was one of those persons so often met with who live what may be termed a well-ordered life. Every morning he rose at 7.30, dressed, breakfasted, and prompt to the minute left his house for the office. So punctual was he that the milkman, postman, and newsboy used him as a watch. Year in and year out Gus always dressed in the same colours – certainly the cut of this suit might change with the fashion but never the colour, which was blue. On his head he always wore a bowler and in his hand an umbrella. At two minutes before 9 am he would enter the office and 5 pm saw him depart. So fixed was his habit that going to and from the office he traversed the same streets and where necessary to cross he always crossed at precisely the same spot. His paper he bought from the same newsboy for years and so true was he to his brand of tobacco that whenever his large frame darkened the door, the tobacconist (a lady) required not to hear the order but made it up at once.

Gus was not averse to taking a dram but never overdid it and, as regards the theatre, Gilbert and Sullivan operas held him as in a trance. I often think with his weight he used to fancy himself a rival to Billington, for it was Billington parts he delighted in humming. Most evenings he spent at home having a room to himself and was usually to be found before a roaring fire either perusing the latest novel or the evening paper.

For years Gus had lived so and then the great war broke out through Europe. Being single there is no doubt that Gus had many a struggle with himself ere "doing his bit" and ultimately, he found himself enrolled in HM Signals.

To those who have never been under discipline the first effects of army life is either to make them or break their hearts. Gus very nearly fell under the latter for at drill such a huge-sized man looks ever so clumsy beside a little one. Consequently the drill instructor had many scathing remarks for Gus's benefit, but as Gus shed his fat so did he become correspondingly smarter till as time rolled on he duly passed out on draft for the front. Never being hurried in his life stood him in good stead for one day when he found himself in what the paper's term "a hot corner", that was practically cut off, Gus stuck to his place and by doing so he saved a whole regiment as he was enabled to inform the General of their predicament. As a result Gus was presented with the DCM before his cheering mates, although a few jealous of him did remark that "He only got it because he was too slow to move from his position fast enough".

The greatest surprise Gus ever sprung on those who knew him was when he got his first leave. His sister declares she will not forget it till her dying day. This surprise which upset all his friends was when on his second day's leave he presented a blushing young lady as Mrs Gus (no other than the tobacconist). Being a bachelor for years before listing nobody dreamed he would ever marry and so his marriage burst on them like a bombshell, but secretly Gus had been worshipping the lady for years. This may explain his habit of always going to the same tobacconist. Many a good and bad habit is not a habit at all when everything is known and revealed.

Gus is again at the front, but he has returned a changed man for now he is always happy. When you ask why he is smiling so, his smile only develops itself but never a word he says. Long may he continue so.

THE BABAHGEE

I am not an aristocrat and therefore can make no comparisons between a Swiss cook, an Irish chef or an Indian cook known as "The Babahgee". Our Babahgee was an Indian, but his ideas of hygiene and cooking were nil. As a cook none of the section would have granted him a tenth-rate certificate, for it was generally understood he would burn water if sent to boil it without supervision. Even with all his faults he still remained with us as cook for he was so untiring in his efforts to please that nobody had the heart to complain about him.

English he could speak well and he considered himself a far-travelled man having been to Port Said and Brighton and back to India, and then to us. He was married but to this day I can't tell to how many wives; I could never fathom if he kept three wives and a sister or three sisters and a wife. Some declared he was soft in the brain, yet one day when sent off with a ten rupee note to buy sugar he returned with a sorrowful tale that he had lost it. Enquiries proved his statement to be correct: he did lose it, but alas, it was by his gambling, and he was duly rewarded with ten strokes of a rattan.

One night our stew was so hot that no one could take it. The Babahgee was cross-examined and it was discovered he had used mustard instead of curry. He was let off through the humorous remark of one of the lads that the Babahgee had done his best to make the stew hot as we were always complaining about it being cold. What race or caste he belongs to I can't say but he declares time and again, "Me's a Christian".

Wood being a scarce commodity it remained a mystery how our Babahgee always had enough. I myself think he had an understanding with some of the Drabbies Carters because when they had a load of wood a piece always dropped off their carts opposite our place and our Babahgee would dart out and secure the valuables. Like us he has a hankering for home but he admits we are very good "sahibs".

MIT

Mit, or to give him his full name, Mitchell, was a typical Scots man except for two things: his great sense of humour and his utter disregard of thriftiness. It seems to be taken for granted by the world that if an individual be Scotch then he must be thrifty, yet throughout my army life I have found that, as regards generosity, Scotch men easily lead first. The "Bang goes another sixpence" theory I have seen exploded time and time again by the cheerfulness of many a Scot in parting quite happily with his bawbees, and not on himself.

While Mit had money he seemed to go on the principle of make merry today for tomorrow we may not have the chance, and he was always open to treat all and sundry. His sense of humour gave us many a hearty laugh for Mit could twist NCOs orders until they became very funny.

Seventeen years married he became a father for the first time two months before enlisting and it is evident that his return home to his family is causing him some uneasiness. An all-round pianist and singer Mit is seen at his best with a wee drappie in and doing a turn at an impromptu concert. A good horseman, a man who takes risks and generous to a fault, many are the friends he has made in the corps and none will say him an ill, truly a position worth more than stars and stripes. Mit's redeeming feature is that he is always in the same humour, never downhearted. Men with this possession count far more than courage to their side for their example has enabled many a painful duty to be done uncomplaining.

TAM

Tam is Scottish and hails from the same part as Mit but they in nature are completely different. Tam's whole life is concentrated on number one – everything is done from the point of view of how it's going to pay him.

    I don't suppose Tam means it, rather watching the main chance for number one has warped his nature till securing the best of everything for himself has become an obsession. However, a good golfer in civil life and a good father I know him to be.

At gambling games Tam is the only one I've known to make it pay; where hundreds would lose their all Tam would come a winner. Tam was not loved by the gambling school because he often caught them on the hop. For instance, one night he lost heavily but the next saw him retrieve his losses and then he retired for the evening. This caused great contention in the school as the losers held it was not a sportsman's action to retire and not give them a chance of revenge. Of course, Tam retorted he'd won enough and "didna want mair."

Tam taken all over was as good as any soldier for he did his share of work without dodging and with a will, which after all is the main thing.

Humour

Two rankers had been given their commission and after celebrating the event, not wisely but too well, were returning to camp when the sentry challenged, "Halt, who goes there?" Supporting each other one replied, "Two damned officers". Like a flash from the sentry came, "Advance two damned officers, all's well".

Even in hospital there was humour. Tommy had been ill for over two weeks, fed on milk only, when the doctor on making his rounds asked him if he thought he could eat an egg. Tommy thought for a minute and then in tones which could be heard right down the ward exclaimed "An egg? Aye, and the blooming hen that laid it!"

The post office attached to our brigade was staffed by Indians and the postmaster was always a source of fun. On one occasion, after a long weary march and before a shot had been fired or even an enemy outpost sighted, he wired to his superior, "Am weary of this warfare, please grant me transfer to a quieter front." On another occasion he was advised that a certain assistant was to be sent to him and although he did not know the man he wired, "Will not accept him. He is a man of bad character." It was pointed out to him he must accept the assistant, and he replied, "Will allow him to come but clearly on the grounds that I accept no responsibility"!

On the banks of the Tigris a certain part of the river was out of bounds to troops. An Indian was caught bathing therein by a British policeman when the following dialogue took place:

> *British Military Policeman:* "Ere, do you understand Hindustani?"
> *Indian:* "Yes Sahib."
> *British Military Policeman (in English):* "Well, blankety blankety blank, off out of this then."

The outpost was held by an Indian regiment and deserters from the Turks were coming in and giving themselves up. One such party approached, and the sentry duly challenged, "Halt! Who goes there. Out of the darkness came in good English, "Turkish deserters." Nobody expected the reply of the sentry, which was, "Advance Turkish deserters and report all well!"

The jackals were howling close to the camp so a new arrival, wondering what it was, turned to a chap who had been some time in the country and asked. "Oh that," replied the old soldier, "is the Mespot nightingale."

On one occasion a General proceeding along the front with his chauffeur made the discovery that the petrol in his car wouldn't be sufficient to carry them. So they stopped, and while the chauffeur was procuring the necessary oil, the General lunched with the officers of the camp. The oil was duly fetched from the supply dump and poured into the tank... the General and his staff took their place in the car, but alas not an inch would the car move. Great was the excitement. The car was put through many tests and after a great waste of time the discovery was made that the contents of the petrol drum supplied by the dump was not petrol but water. There was no hope but for the General to content himself till real petrol was put in the tank. In spite of investigation no solution was ever found as to how water came to be in the drum though it was generally put down to a case of scrounge.

One day Tom Jones received a parcel from home. In the section all parcels were shared by the community, but Jones could find no one who would accept of the contents of his parcel as it contained about a dozen bottles all carefully packed and containing, according to their labels, cough mixture. On the arrival of the parcel it was remarked how appropriate was its delivery as poor Tom developed a bad cough necessitating resource to his cough mixtures daily. Tom had been curing himself with his mixture for about three days when one of his chums accidently got a smell of his breath, after which everybody partook of the cough mixture which happened to be the very best Scotch whisky.

The palm for unconscious humour I think should go to one of the Arab sheikhs (head man). This particular individual refused to pay certain dues and refused to comply with certain orders. He was proclaimed an outlaw and troops were sent to subdue his tribe. When the sheikh saw that the British were in earnest he sent the following request to the army authorities: "Please withdraw your artillery and all your machine guns, and I think I can then beat you man to man"!

To the question, "What won the war?" some wit had replied "Woodbines!" The true answer would take much thought to discover but there can be no dispute that a great factor was the keen sense of humour possessed by the British army.

Often have I wished that the Gods of Fate had endowed me with the art of drawing in black and white scenes that I have witnessed. Many a good yarn has been told and many a good drawing made of humorous incidents of the war, but countless incidents have gone unrecorded, incidents which – had anyone been able to portray on paper – would have sent the world laughing for many a day.

On joining up I was fully prepared for a very hard, dour sort of experience but before I was a day in HM Forces I discovered that below all the nightmare of making a fighting machine out of raw material it was the sense of humour that kept the game going.

The recruit squad had been busy forming fours, right and left inclines, till they were weary and sick of it. At this point the instructor called a halt and addressing the squad desired to know if any man understood motorcycles. To the envy of the squad one bright youth with visions of a joy ride stepped forward. Sergeant Instructor enquired, "Well my man, do you thoroughly understand the motorbike?" To which the youth responded, "Oh yes, sir!" Sergeant Instructor answered, "Well hop over to the officers' quarters and clean Captain Thingamabobs bike!"

On one occasion a brigade had to withdraw. It was a sad blow to the men, but orders had to be obeyed. Arrangements had been made and the withdrawal had to begin. The advance party had marched for about three hours when on emerging from a side road the discovery was made that they had, instead of marching away from the position, gone around in a circle and were once again at the starting point. Disgust was felt by everybody when suddenly a cockney voice was heard to exclaim in sorrowful tones "Ere Bill, ain't we bin asked to do lots of funny things in this ere army?" Out of the darkness came the reply, "That's so Joe." Even the enraged General had to laugh for Joe's voice continued "Well blimey, ain't this the first time they've asked us to loop the blinkin loop!" The withdrawal continued in a cheerful mood.

Even under shell fire a sense of humour never deserted

the men. I know of one company in the trenches which kept a record of the shells. A "dud" being put down as made by such and such a firm, one fairly far off to be quite safe, and the real dangerous ones to a firm the head of which was particularly good to the company in gifts. Needless to say, all the firms mentioned were of the town from which the company came.

The Bus Horse

The bus horse was one of the few animals I can say I was comfortable on. He came to us with a bunch and at first was put down as being lazy, but this was a libel on his character for it was our lack of his way which, luckily, we soon tumbled to.

He was cumbersome, having been employed as an inside wheeler of a gun carriage. The result of this was before he would move a step the military orders q*uick march*, w*alk march*, or *gallop* had to be given, and seldom did he stop unless called on to *halt*.

He was frightened at nought except camels which put a terrible fear on him. From his style he was christened the 'bus'.

Before he left us, he was in fine sleek condition. We had to part with him when we moved as he was an extra.

Army Hospital

Of all the jobs in the army, hospital ward orderly is the last I would think of going after. Such a job requires almost a superhuman, for 10–12 hours a day he is forever on the move. His duties are legion and include washing patients, changing beds, dishing up the medicine, fetching food and acting as general servant to all and sundry. From morning to night he keeps smiling and the only difference he knows to his job is whether he is under a good, bad, or indifferent sister.

When you enter hospital and go into your ward the sister becomes your mother for the time being. She is usually pretty indulgent but at the same time watches you observe the rules and regulations. To some it would appear all she did was take temperatures and restrict diets but bless your heart it's her work. The climate out here must try her, yet she always keeps merry and bright before her patients.

We have two Gurkha orderlies. Their duty is to deliver messages within walking distance of the office. They are supposed to take turn about but for the life of us it is hardly possible to tell one from the other. It is a sort of Box and Cox comedy with them. Both are the same height, features alike, and always spick and span for the Gurkha is easily the smartest and cleanest dressed we possess. If you ask if they are brothers they laugh heartily and answer, "No sahib," for they are not even relatives. Both are favourites for they are always merry and bright and extraordinarily energetic in performance of their duties.

The Indian Navy

My first taste of navigation conducted entirely by Indian natives was at Bombay. The thing driven by steam on which I got my introduction was what some would call a ship-come-ferry, others a tender, but the natives who manned it were convinced of it being Dreadnought. Dreadnought it certainly seemed to me by the miraculous way they had of just missing obstacles such as liners lying at anchor buoys, fishing smacks and what not.

As a sailor the Indian is passable, only discipline as known in the English navy seems unknown. On a ticklish point of navigation arising all and sundry tender advice to the captain. On one occasion I remember there was difficulty about the approach of a tender to a transport and while the tender drifted with the current the whole crew, including the stokers from the interior and the cabin boys, were arguing the toss about how to get it up to the lines. A row arose among them and peace was only restored by the skipper laying about them with a belaying pin.

These sailors mix business with their calling and are always ready to sell you fruit and cigarettes which they seem to produce from nowhere. They appear to be highly pleased with their occupation and are extra patriotic.

Uqbah

On returning to Ramadi from Khan Baghdadi we had not settled down long when my brigade took over the line of communications halfway to Hit. John Air and myself were despatched to take over the furthest-up office which was Uqbah, the idea being that all our section would take it in turns to do a month on this work. You will look in vain for Uqbah on a map of Mespot unless you happen to have an official army map, for at Uqbah there is no city or town.

This camp was situated about 25 miles north of Ramadi and was the halfway resting place for all convoys except mechanical, which of course did the journey from Hit to Ramadi in one day. At Uqbah there was no necessity to sigh for the solitude of the desert for it was there all right. The camp was on the riverbank, just a little below where the river emerged from a high rocky gorge, and it was also flanked by a high double ridge of sand. South, east and west for miles on end there was nothing but sandy desert, but to the north there was a high rocky barren ridge. Such was the scenery of Uqbah.

In the camp itself there was only about a dozen white people, consisting of the camp commandant, a British officer, the IWT representative, a sergeant of the supplies and two or three artillery men in charge of an ammunition dump. Though in a quiet place life at Uqbah was very exciting. Not far off was an Arab village every now and then, in spite of vigilant sentries, the Arab would succeed in stealing goods from the supply dump. How they did it will I think always be a mystery but by some method or another many bags of atta (flour) would be stolen and only detected in the light of morning. One theory of their success held that the Arabs creep up to the place in a line with about a hundred yards between each man. When the thief succeeds in securing a bag he crawls back to the next Arab who repeats the process till the man furthest off has possession. This line extends far enough to be out of the sentry's vision and hearing, where the stolen goods can then be placed on a waiting donkey or camel and successfully taken away.

During the time I was on the post it was garrisoned by a company of the 1/5th Gurkhas, who were most vigilant fellows. The camp as I have said had a double sand ridge on the west and the road leading into the camp from the highway, about a quarter of a mile off, was guarded by a sentry who patrolled on the top of the ridge nearest the camp. The wind, strange to say, as a rule blew over the ridges and across the camp with the result that when the sentry challenged anyone approaching by the road his shout of *halt* was seldom heard. One night at dusk a Gurkha returning from the latrine, which was over the second ridge for sanitary reasons, was challenged by the sentry. No answer. After another "Halt, who goes there?" there was a second dead silence, the sentry opened fire, and the fun began. The whole camp rushed out to their prearranged places and when it was discovered the cause of the alarm was one of their own men they didn't half enjoy the joke. Although I don't understand the Gurkha's language I saw sufficient to pity the poor sentry for he got unmercifully chaffed for a few days over the incident. I may say that after this happening I would not venture outside the camp after dark…

On another occasion a certain sheikh, having failed to pay

certain dues, was arrested. He was duly brought to Uqbah and placed inside the wire enclosure with a guard outside. This was about midday. Towards evening an Arab on a raft covered high with brushwood came floating down the river. Being suspicious of this craft the IWT chap challenged the Arab, who put into the riverbank. As he had no pass and could not state his business he was put under arrest and placed in the enclosure with the sheikh. That very night the sentry caught the pair in the act of making their escape and although he fired and raised the alarm both made away. On investigation it was discovered that the rickety old craft which had been moored to the bank had also disappeared. Next morning a detachment went out and searched for the sheikh at his village a few miles off. Without finding any trace of their man they brought back all the livestock as security from the village.

The sequel to this affair was that all the livestock had to be returned to the village except a few head of sheep equivalent to the sum due by the sheikh, with no further action taken. The British scored because the sheep were killed and issued as rations, a very delightful change to tinned meat.

There was communication to Hit from Ramadi and the south by the river as well as by road. On the river a special kind of boat was employed known as the F-boats. These and bellums carried many tons of goods such as food, ammunition, and clothing, as well as bitumen and lime which were found in large qualities around Hit. The navigation of the river was at times a very exciting occupation as the boats were often sniped at by the Arabs from the banks. A village about 3 miles below Uqbah was notorious for this sort of thing and one night we were alarmed to hear machine gun fire. It was pitch-dark and soon the rays of an F-boat's searchlight could be seen downstream. The F-boat came up and moored at our camp, the skipper asking if there was a surgeon on the post stating he had two men wounded. The surgeon was duly fetched but the skipper on seeing him refused to allow the surgeon on his ship and cast off, proceeding up stream to Hit. It transpired afterwards that the boat had been fired on by the Arabs and the crew had replied with their machine gun (all F-boats had one mounted on deck). Two of the crew had been hit but their wounds were more scratches.

At this part of the river there were shoals of fish and the Gurkhas used to make fishing lines. They were successful in landing many large catches, one in particular being a fish about four feet long.

While I was at Uqbah I was sent for to go on furlough but the journey from there will make a story for another day.

Furlough

For furlough the Mespot front was badly served. Owing to the submarine danger and, according to the head, a "lack of shipping", furlough to England was out of the question, and so those of us who were fortunate enough to get furlough had to go to India. Personally I didn't mind this because having come so far I desired to see India before returning home. Besides I had no desire to get home until I knew I would never have to leave again.

It was supposed to be the rule that only those who had been abroad over 18 months were entitled to furlough, but this was not strictly adhered to. Many men entitled never got any leave whilst others, only a few months out, were fortunate enough to get leave.

I was at Uqbah when my turn came. Not being on good terms with the sergeant I was left to make my own arrangements for reaching headquarters, some 28 miles away from Uqbah. I was very chummy with the chap in charge of the IWT. and he said he would get me a passage on one of the boats going downstream. As luck would have it a bellum arrived and was loaded up with shells from the dump at Uqbah, which was being withdrawn. On this ship I travelled down to headquarters at Ramadi. On that short river trip I think I got more excitement than all the rest of my furlough wanderings. To begin with we had only been an hour on our way when the boat sprang a leak. As soon as this was discovered the boatmen, all Arabs, manoeuvred the ship to the water's edge and began to repair it. The method was indeed surprising. They used no joiners' tools but, taking off what scanty clothes they did wear, they dived down the side of the ship. Each Arab as he dived carried a chunk of mud and grass mixed, and with this plugged the hole. After an hour or so spent at this performance the ship was again watertight and our journey restarted. However, the boatmen had calculated up the time and had decided that they would not go further than Ramadi although due at Dhibban that day.

One of the rules of the river forbid travelling after dark and so our boatmen began to make sure of not reaching Ramadi till nightfall. Although there was a favourable wind blowing instead of taking advantage of it they continually ran aground on sandbanks, on one occasion of grounding close to the bank they made no attempt to get off but began to light a fire on board, right above the shells, with the intention of cooking a meal. However the artillery chaps in charge had seen enough of it and they set about the Arabs with the butt end of their rifles and soon had the ship underway again. After much fighting, swearing and bumping we arrived about nightfall at Ramadi having spent practically a whole day on the river upon a journey which could easily have been done in a couple of hours.

The company motor took us down on a Sunday morning, the 10th of June, to Dhibban. The journey down was uneventful and uninteresting, the scenery being simply sand desert as far as the eye could see except for a few palm trees on the riverbank. Dhibban, which means in Arabic *the land of the sharp-toothed fly*, is well named. Sand flies abound in the thousands making sleep almost an impossibility and the rest camp at which we stayed till Monday night was one of the worst I have ever experienced. Our journey to Basra was done by stages in the following order: Dhibban to Baghdad by rail, across the Tigris by ferry to Hinaidi, from there to Kut by rail, Kut to Amara by river steamer and Amara to Margil (Basra) by rail. By the time I reached Basra my mind was made up that if the war should last twenty years, I would never again undergo such conditions of travel. The railway journeys were done in open trucks and so thickly packed were we that it was impossible to get even a decent rest far less a sleep. Not only were we overcrowded but the nights were very cold, and all railway journeys were done between 11 pm and 6 am. The trucks we travelled in were not prepared in any way for our reception. Once we got a night in a coal truck and when we finished the journey the British had to wash before we could be distinguished from natives. The river steamer was better than railway for one could get lain down, though there was hardly any space between the sleeping figures to walk on.

At Barsa we expected to be held up for a few days as the previous draft which left our company had been held there a week and kept busy loading and unloading barges because of a local labour strike. However, our good fortune continued and we were sent aboard the steamer Elephanta and sailed about 10 am. The voyage from Barsa to Bombay took five days. It was the monsoon season and although no gale struck us the gulf was very rough. The heat was sickening. The heat in the Persian Gulf is very peculiar, it makes you sweat but the perspiration it draws out like syrup, very sticky and although bathes be taken every hour the stickiness remains. It is so bad that by placing the palm of your hand on the top of your head you can raise all the hairs.

The Elephanta is a good enough sea boat but, on this

occasion, I think it carried representatives of all the East. There were Indians of all castes and a large number of Anglo-Indians too. These Anglo-Indians were going either on furlough or returning to India because their terms of contract with the railway in Mespot had finished. Their contract amused me. Every one of them appeared to have a couple of large trunks and a deck chair and although the ship was very crowded these chaps seemed to think they were entitled to about two thirds of the whole ship. In fact, their whole attitude was as if they were Lords of Creation. During the voyage I had conversations with many of these chaps. Some were very interesting but all of them struck me as thinking they were little tin gods.

I hated most their attitude to the Indians. I've seen soldiers who have done long spells in India treat Indians pretty rough, but their roughness was kindness compared with what the Anglo-Indian served out.

On board the ship was a large number of Japanese. These were tradesmen such as carpenters returning to Japan. Apparently the British government paid them very good wages and they signed on for six months at a time. These chaps interested me very much. They took up their quarters in the gangway along the engine room. All their luggage seemed to consist of was a grass mat and an opium pipe. They fed late at night on rice and seemed to spend the rest of their time smoking opium, especially through the night, for often the fumes of these pipes would reach us who slept on deck, and it was not a nice perfume. All the time on board the Elephanta there seemed to be a peculiar odour, something similar to a cattle boat. A chum of mine who was travelled much said it was always like that where large numbers of Eastern people are carried.

How is it that gambling thrives so well on-board ship? On the Elephanta all the different races seemed to be engaged in killing time and thought by gambling. Certainly, the games differed but the ends were the same. The Japanese gamble with a board of squares and round pieces, whilst the British and Indians took to cards.

As our ship steamed into dock it was not the buildings that proved of most interest but a couple of white waitresses. They were serving in a building on the quay in a restaurant, the front of which was open. Practically all eyes of the British soldiers of all ranks were fixed on these two girls, a very human sign, for some of these men had seen no ladies for over two years.

Of Bombay I regret I can write very little but what I did see was sufficient to convince me it was no great place as a residence for British people. Bombay I think looks best from the sea. Its spires, domes and buildings look most imposing from that point of view. We were taken off the boat and put in a large warehouse, waited there for about an hour, and then got into our railway train which was brought to the door of the warehouse. The docks of Bombay are just the same as docks all over the world: plenty of bustle and smell. I have often read of the beautiful blending of colours in Indian towns, but alas I saw not its beauty. Bombay colours especially in the dresses of the natives were varied enough but somehow gave no pleasure to the eye and I have yet to discover wherein lies the beauty of the East. From Bombay I travelled by troop train to Poona, my depot. The journey was done by night. Night travelling for soldiers seems to be the mania with the army for only on one occasion have I travelled by day and that because the journey was one of three days and nights.

Leaving Bombay we passed through some very remarkable districts but on gaining open country it was a feast for the Gods. For miles could be seen vegetation of a dark green and looking out of the carriage window I felt I could go on looking on such beauty for ages. Really it was like a drink of cold water when parched with thirst, especially after months of desert wandering.

India is a vast continent and has many miles of railway but the hundred odd miles of railway from Bombay to Poona are amongst the finest railways of the world, especially for mountain scenery. The line goes up and over the Ghats and this track is an everlasting monument to British engineering skill. The line tunnels through rocks at many places and often the track is on a ledge with only about a couple of feet clear of the edge. At one such place if you look out of the carriage window you see, thousands of feet straight down below, the tops of trees in a valley, and if you cross the carriage and look out at the other side you see only a blank wall. By putting your head out of the window you can look up the side of the mountain for thousands of feet almost straight into the air. Two engines are required to pull the train up this part of the railway.

On the train I travelled with there was a very sad happening. A young lad sprang off the seat of the carriage right through the open window. He did it so quickly nobody was prepared to stop him. The train was stopped, and the poor lad's body found cut in two. He was very popular with the chaps who were with him, and I learned that on coming off the ship his foot had slipped on the gangway down to the well deck and he fell and hurt his head. He was seen by a doctor in Bombay but the lad had declared he felt alright so was not detained in hospital. Poor fellow, the fall must have affected his brain. The guard of the train was not a bit shocked at the occurrence as he said such affairs were getting quite common on this particular part of the line. In fact, he stated this was the third case of jumping through the window during that summer. I arrived at Poona about 2 am and for that night our draft was placed in tents.

POONA

Poona is a delightful spot. It is high above sea level in a very densely wooded part of the country. In fact, so thick are the trees that on looking down on the country from Parbetti Temple (a Hindu Temple on a high hill) nothing can be seen of the buildings of Poona as they are completely hidden by the foliage. I was at Poona during the best season for the weather was exactly similar to our own British summers and all the time I was there I had more the idea that I was on Deeside instead of India.

Poona is a town with a long historic record. It dates as far back as 1700 but in spite of its antiquity in many things it seems to have made no progress. For instance, its sanitation must be pretty much the same today as it has been for hundreds of years past. The sanitary system of Poona is one of its blights. All the house sewage is collected in bullock-drawn carts which amble along with their collection to a sewage farm outside the town. As they jostle along the sewage gets jerked out in big splashes on the roadway. In course of time traffic reduces it to dust which becomes scattered when the wind blows, and yet we wonder why India has so many epidemics and plagues. To meet these carts is an effective method of completely spoiling a whole day's pleasure as their perfume is a thing that once experienced makes any mortal go miles out of his way rather than encounter again.

Poona is not like any hometown. The only street similar to streets in British towns is the one wherein is the bazaar. Here the buildings are right on the street and all are shops occupied by Indians. Elsewhere lie the European business houses or residences; the buildings are well off the roadway having large grounds in front usually with plenty trees.

It was the society season and during my visit the Governor of Bombay, Lord Wellington, and his suite were in residence. Also it was the horse racing season. In one of his books Kipling hints that horse racing in India is a shady business. Now I am no authority on horse racing but two incidents I witnessed at the Poona racecourse has convinced me that Kipling is right. The first incident was in a race in which I was partner of a sweepstake ticket on a certain horse. This horse came successfully round the dangerous bend well in the lead when quite evident to everybody the jockey began to pull... the crowd on the stands hissed but that horse lost its lead and the race. The other incident was at the starting point. I went to get a snapshot of a race start and in this particular race was a jockey who had done extra well in the previous day's racing. When he got up to the tape the starter ordered him back to come up again, as soon as the jockey had turned his horse and was two lengths away, while his back was to the tape, the starter set the race off. Of course the jockey hadn't a ghostly chance though he made a great attempt, from which it was evident that given a fair start he stood a good chance.

The racecourse grounds at Poona are very good but just at the last turn to the winning post there is a very dangerous bend. A watch tower affair has been erected wherein stands an umpire to see that no tactics contrary to the rules are indulged in by the racers. At this bend many accidents have happened. One jockey was badly hurt while I was there. He was reported dead in the evening, but it proved false as the man was fit again before the season's end. In case of further accidents, a wise management supplied a motor ambulance on the course, and it did seem peculiar to watch a race followed at a respectable distance by a red cross motor ambulance.

In Poona as elsewhere the soldier's welfare was left entirely to the YMCA and here it did it very well indeed. To the YMCA I was indebted to hearing Lord Wellington speak. His address on the work and activities of the organisation was well thought out, clearly put and well delivered. Pale-looking with dark hair and of quiet demeanour nevertheless it was evident he had a telling personality. Lady Wellington is beyond my description. She came with several other ladies of generals and so on to a YMCA social evening. Her Ladyship was a great organiser on behalf of the troops in Mespot. As soon as she entered the Indians of great height and dressed in royal uniform of red took up their position on guard at the door with loaded pistols. I must say that if all the ladies in the land did as the ladies at this social then there would be less class hatred. Although only common soldiers these ladies mixed and spoke with us as if we were equals in station. I can't recall any precise words, but I do know they spoke of the war and seemed always to strike topics interesting to speaker and listener. After the first shock had worn off, I remember thinking to myself what a great institution our aristocracy was. After all, it was really worth fighting for if only to assure that such beautiful people should live. As a race is it not the thought that in time we rise higher in social scale and that helps us to keep our nose to the grindstone of life?

In all Indian towns there is the native's part and the European part. Of the native part of Poona I can say but little. What I did see of it left me thinking that there were worse places on earth than our British town slums.

Poona is purely a residential town but for a quiet holiday it is an ideal place. It has cinema theatres but has a lovely public garden, the Empress, in which all kinds of eastern trees are growing. There is always a fly in the ointment and Poona's fly is cholera. Outbreaks of this disease is common.

Shopping in the bazaar is great sport and entirely different from shopping at home. When you desire anything at home you look at the shop windows to see the article, note its price and buy it if you want to. In the bazaar there are no shop windows; the goods are in the shop. You enter, take up the article you desire and ask the price. If you are experienced you halve the shopkeeper's price and offer that, then you start a series of bidding and bargaining. The end is usually that the shopkeeper will offer to toss you, if you win you pay your price if he wins you pay his price. The price is fixed either way, however, and leaves him a good profit. I remember being strong on two ivory carvings. The price demanded was 200 rupees. I would not give the sum and seeing I was not keen the dealer produced an identical pair of ivory figures offering them for only 45 rupees. To the uninitiated there was no difference in the figures, only the price. It certainly requires skill and knowledge to shop in India.

TRAVELLING IN INDIA

On arrival at Poona our hopes of a great holiday in India were shattered. We were paraded before the OC of the depot and politely told there was little chance of our getting further than the depot as, owing to the misbehaviour of some Australians in Calcutta, it had been decided to curtail all furlough except to places under army supervision. As only one per cent of accommodation was allowed to Signals, we might as well decide to spend our leave in Poona. As every one of us had come on furlough with our plans laid as to where and how we were to spend our leave, great dissatisfaction was felt with this announcement. Give them their due however, the authorities at Poona gave furlough men in the depot absolute free rope. We could go anywhere without pass except into the areas always out of bounds and, being placed in a camp on our own, there was no restriction on our going and coming after 2 pm. One could remain out to any hour of the night.

The only thing we were called upon to do was to provide a guard, but this was easy, one being a sort of watch in case of any thieving or disturbance. The guard was brought about because one furlough man had been drinking heavily and boasting of the number of rupees he had in his belt. He was taken to camp one night very drunk and somebody used a jack knife to cut the belt from his body, cutting his stomach instead from which wounds the victim died… this incident remained a mystery until one of the men implicated gave himself up and turned King's evidence.

Well as I said it looked very much as if I'd spend my furlough in Poona and as I intended visiting friends (Mr and Mrs Dalgarno) at Cawnpore I sent them word. My luck was in: Mr Dalgarno brought influence to bear, and I was allowed to proceed to Cawnpore. I was not given the opportunity of travelling on my own but was sent on a special troop train. It took me days to do the journey from Poona to Cawnpore. At times the train would travel for hours at around 60 miles an hour then after a spell of this high speed we would spend hours on a siding.

The railways of India are nothing like home trains. Of course, it is quite evident that the accommodation must differ for slow though some of our own railway systems are no journey extends into night and day. In India on the long distance trains the compartments are built so that sleeping accommodation is provided. This is done by having the seats placed along each side of the carriage and a folding shelf can be let down which forms another bed. The windows are triple: a glass one, then a venetian blind made of wood, and another of metal perforated by small holes. These are for weather conditions. The compartments are various. Some for families, others for ladies only, and of course carriages for Whites only and Blacks only.

The railway stations throughout India are all dismal but the tracks are very well kept indeed. The whole of the European carriages are finely and comfortably fitted with cushions. The system seems to be run by Anglo-Indians and taken on the whole the servants of the Indian Railways are an insolent lot.

The journey up country from Poona to Jhansi Junction is over flat country and the thing that surprised me most was the huge tracts of waste land we passed through. Probably the land is only fit to lie barren, but it struck me that surely agriculture had advanced sufficiently to make this waste land of use. As we went along, we could see farming in progress but here there were no steam ploughs or reapers. Cultivation of the land is carried out today in India much as it has been done for hundreds of years past. One reason for this is that the average Indian does not like to use modern methods and also, owing to the caste system, Indians of one caste wont work on land of another caste thus making the labour problem acute. Possibly too the land laws have something to do with it, but these will make for a story another day. The wooden plough drawn by oxen and crops cut by knife are still the order of the day.

Taken all over the rolling stock of the railways are very good. The short journey trains can compare with English trains as regards travelling comfort. The laws of travel, however, require to be seriously overhauled. I have seen many as 20 Indians in a second-class carriage built to hold 18. This crowding wouldn't be so bad, but passengers are allowed much more luggage than would be tolerated in a home compartment. This crowd of 20 had taken into the carriage heaps of personal luggage and as each had a large basket, and the day was hot, you can draw your own picture of the comfort. Of course, this only applies to the Indian population – the more they get crowded into a carriage the happier the authorities seem to be. Travelling by rail in India is very cheap but the amount of comfort you get depends on your colour, and also your social standing.

On my return journey from Cawnpore to Jhonsie I had to travel in a first class compartment. The fault was not mine. All the carriages were occupied by Indians and, as the first-class compartments were empty, on appealing to the guard permission was granted to travel therein. It was a nice journey and I arrived in Jhonsie at midnight. My connection to Poona was by the Delhi Express and as that train was not due till 7 am like a rude soldier I laid me down to sleep on the station seat. I was just beautifully away to the land of nod when I was awakened by an Indian ticket collector who demanded to know why I travelled from Cawnpore in a first class with a second class warrant. I told him the reason and went off to sleep again. Just as I once more got into grip of Morpheus I was knocked out again by another railway official demanding the same answer to the previous question. This went on every time I tried to sleep until I think every official from the station master downwards had interviewed me. The upshot was my name, number and regiment were taken and I was told for my offence I would have to pay 40 rupees which, needless to say, I have not yet been called upon to pay.

Graft in its keenest Yankees sense plays a great game on the Indian railroad and the bigger the tip the greater the things one can do. The meals provided at the station hotels and buffets throughout India were good but so was the price demanded while liquid refreshments were so dear that even had I desired them the price was beyond my pocket.

Major General Sir Henry Havelock

CAWNPORE

Cawnpore is situated in a well wooded country. As elsewhere in India the European population live in districts known as cantonments, each house standing in its own grounds. The city is full of historical interest, its places being famed through the mutiny of 1857. I spent a most delightful holiday for which my thanks are due to Mr and Mrs Dalgarno who were extremely kind to me. Mr Dalgarno when off duty took me about in his motorcycle and side car. I saw all the famous places of the mutiny and my host being well versed in all the incidents of that time had that great gift of being able to describe things till one could actually fancy them taking place in reality, which made my visit ever so much more interesting.

I remember one evening we went to the Khata. The sun was

setting on the river and a hush was over everything. On the top of one of the jetties were a few soldiers of the fresh regiment stationed at Cawnpore. We sat down near them, and my host began to relate to me the history and the part played in it by this building. One of the soldiers, catching our topic, asked Mr Dalgarno if he had any objection to giving his address to the crowd and as Mr Dalgarno had none, we circled round him and listened spell bound to the story. One may read and think they know and understand all about historical events but never before had the Indian mutiny and its effect been so impressed upon me as when I visited these places.

As an Aberdonian naturally I was surprised to find at Cawnpore two gentlemen of the name Pirie, sons of an Aberdeen university professors who had fallen in the Cawnpore Massacre. A bronze plate records the fact in the memorial Church. One day Mr Dalgarno took me through to Lucknow by the motorcycle and side car. We crossed the Ganges by a bridge across which traffic was only allowed in one direction. The bridge is almost one and a half miles long and only wide enough for a carriage and two bodies to pass along, running parallel with it is a similar bridge which carries the traffic in the other direction. The distance from Cawnpore to Lucknow is about 50 miles and except for a few miles out of Cawnpore and a few near Lucknow the road is one of the best I've ever been on. It is almost straight and on each side of the roadway trees grow. These trees have a double use. First, they give shade to the roadway from the sun and second, they form a source of revenue to the government. The ride along the road was delightful. We passed through a few villages. At each village there is a place where travellers (Indian) have to put up at sunset. No travellers are allowed on the road after dark, a precautionary measure to keep down dacoity (thieving). Monkeys are numerous on this road. The little beggars would scurry across the road in front of us and then scramble up a tree and hanging down from a branch would look after us with a very impertinent look. Buffaloes didn't take kindly to our method of locomotion and often after we passed we could see one of them chasing down after us.

We stopped at the Alambagh. In this garden is the grave of Major General Sir Henry Havelock and to this day the marks and holes made by the cannonballs of the rebels can be seen. Lucknow seemed like a dream. At the residency we were taken in hand by the army pensioner there. He is the official guide to the place and his appearance made me think of an old English squire. From a model in the hall, we could see exactly how things were during the days of the great mutiny. Being Scottish of course I had to see the room wherein Jessie had her dream. The place was duly pointed out but how the number of women managed to live even for one day in such a confined and badly ventilated room is beyond my comprehension. We visited numerous temples and art galleries including the famous Chota Imambara, the palace of the million lights. When I was at Lucknow it was very warm and I formed the opinion that the heat of that part of India is harder on one than the heat of Mespot. In Lucknow I also saw my first elephant in India.

Probably I am wrong but, somehow, I have formed the idea that the British people in India, especially in the old famous mutiny places, have not yet got a feeling of security. Of course, no one said so in words, but hints here and there have given me the idea that the European people do not trust the Indian of today and would not be surprised at a rising. Events have gone that way since I have been there although to all appearance everything is again normal. I believe India will require to be ruled in a different fashion in the future.

Khan Baghdadi

The battle of Khan Baghdadi took place between the 27th and 29th March 1918, and it was a huge success. Our casualties only numbered 31 including two killed while the Turks suffered heavily. We captured over 5,000 men and 15 guns and all the enemy munitions. As a result of this victory the Turks practically ceased to exist on the Euphrates front.

We were at Ramadi when orders were issued for a three-day reconnaissance in the enemy's country. Practically all our brigade went out and after two days it was decided to begin the preliminaries of another attack on the enemy. The British army is slow to get going but once it starts it moves very fast. We spent days at Khan Abu Ryat, about 18 miles from Ramadi, until sufficient supplies were brought up and this place was made the supply dump for the operations which had Hit as its objective. From Rayat we moved to Uqbah and back again to Rayat several times. The distance was only about 10 miles but many a grouse was made at the performance. It did seem ridiculous to keep a brigade moving up and down, but it was all part I believe of a plan to hoodwink the enemy.

When at Ramadi we were often visited by enemy aeroplanes, but it was at Uqbah where I got my first experience of being bombed from above. A pal and I had gone down to the river for the purpose of filling our water bottles and having a wash. Fortunately the river had very steep banks and while we were in the act of filling our bottles an enemy aeroplane came over the camp and dropped bombs. At once the machine guns opened fire and the plane crossed right over where my pal and I were. We got right in the line of the machine gun bullets. We were safe enough, however, as the high steep bank gave us ample protection. A few weeks later at the same place an enemy plane came along and dropped a bomb. It killed two men of the Oxfords and a curious thing was that there were three of them in company but one, wanting to light a cigarette, stood up to do so while his chums walked on. They were killed but he escaped. Reprisals were made on the enemy at Hit for these air raids on us. Our planes began one night at 10 pm and kept up bombing the enemy at intervals of half an hour right on till 5 am next morning.

It was bitterly cold and a full moon. Lying where we were we could hear the explosions of the bombs as they were dropped. We could also hear the aeroplane engines as they passed on their mission and we would lie counting the explosions, knowing that each plane dropped eight. There is humour everywhere. The last airman on his return, on reaching over our camp, signalled on his hooter, "Be not afraid. Cheerio."

From Uqbah we set out to take the town of Hit. Hit was a disappointment, for the enemy had evacuated their positions and we took possession without any opposition. Hit is situated in a district absolutely oozing with bitumen. It literally oozes out of the ground and even comes up in the riverbed. The smell it gives the country may be healthy but is most objectionable, being like a smell from a mammoth sewer. Hit itself looks a promising town from the distance being perched on a sloping upland. For miles distant a tower in the town can be seen and as you approach the district the city looks very well, but alas only from the external view is the town charming. Inside it is a filthy place with narrow streets and sanitation sufficient to raise any kind of plague.

Why the Turks ever evacuated the defences of Hit is a mystery. They were absolutely the best I've seen. Before you approach within two miles of the town you have to pass through a fairly large gorge. At one time the river must have flowed through here; the roadway was such as to give me that impression, with sand and pebbles worn smooth and looking as if they had been polished by running water. From each side of this gorge the Turks had built trenches, dugouts, and so on, and I am certain that had we been the possessors of such a position we would never have been driven out. At Hit we remained a few more days for the same reason as at Ryat, the bringing up of sufficient supplies. General Brooking was in command, and if all the generals were like him Britain would be well served indeed. He always studied his men with the result that his division would tackle anything he proposed and do so cheerfully.

From Hit we moved to Sahillyah and from here we set out for the attack on Khan Baghdadi. The order of the day issued by the general was "March hard and hit hard", and we did it. Our unit left camp about 10 pm and as it was then dark and the roads thick with traffic, progress was slow, and many halts had to be made. After a time, however our column fell into its place and one great adventure had begun.

We had marched for a few hours and then at about 3 am we could distinguish far away in the distance the flare of Verey lights and the rumble of heavy fire. It was all very weird. Here we were marching along, everyone as silent as could be, no smoking or speaking being allowed, with the rumble of heavy guns away in the distance. I really thought it was our own artillery which was firing at this time; I only discovered it was the Turks after the game was over.

At daybreak our column was halted. We had only been a few minutes at rest when a high explosive shell came and burst not 200 yards off. This was followed by several others, luckily all short. High explosive shells are very interesting. They come with a heavy boring sough and when they explode send up a large cloud of black smoke and tons of earth. A few seconds elapse after the shell strikes before the explosion and many a time we were "Had", for the Turks seemed to fire a large number of duds.

As things became rather hot we were shifted back so that we were out of range. It was a pontoon bridge crowd on our left that Johnnie had been trying to shell but I think he failed to do much damage. The most vivid recollection of that day was my own condition. After marching all night when we stopped the cold seemed to affect me cruelly: my whole body was stiff, hands red and teeth chattering. Most of us were in a like condition and also hungry. True, we had a cup of tea shortly after halting, but as it was made the previous day and had been placed in a special vacuum sort of receptacle, it was almost cold when served and tasted so bad few were able to drink it. Seeing our condition our second sergeant got permission to issue half of an emergency rum ration, and I must say that it put new life into me. In fact, with the heat of the sun and the effects of the rum, though only a small dose, by midday I had gone to the other extremes and was too warm.

At this point we remained till 10 am when further orders were issued. As far as I could make out our column, Dorsets and two Gurkha regiments had to make a detour and attack a position called Q.

We set off about 11 am and kept marching until we reached the point (Brookings Whadi) from which our attack was to be made.

A Wadhi is a deep sort of gorge cut by the water off the plains as it drains to the river. These Whadis are usually full of water in the rainy season, but dry in the summer. Just before we reached Brookings Whadi we had to descend from a high hill and cross an open plain. As soon as we got on the plain Johnnie started to shell us with shrapnel. I don't think anybody gets time to be frightened when under fire. True, you wonder if you are to be hurt, but when you hear a shell go whistling overhead, you laugh. Why I don't know, unless it is the humour of being missed that tickles the fancy. As we were going along suddenly a shell burst right in front of our section and everybody threw themselves on the ground. We had a miraculous escape for none of us had even a scratch.

I think the Turks had mistaken the cable wagon on our left for a gun, and so narrow was our escape that when this shell burst and we all ducked, the operator on the cable cart expected to see at least a few of us knocked out and got quite a surprise when he saw us rise and all continue to march.

On arriving at Brookings Whadi, our general found that his men would have to cross an open plain before reaching the Q position and it was decided to bombard it and lay down a barrage. Fortunately I was with Headquarters and as the general and staff had taken up a position from which the whole enemy's position could be seen I saw all the bombardment.

The position was in a sort of hill and was shaped like the top of a cottage loaf. Our artillery fire was magnificent. They seemed to make a complete circle round the position with high explosives and in the centre of this circle they fired smaller shells. In about five minutes after opening fire that position was like a hill on fire. Clouds of smoke rose from it. This was kept up for about 20 minutes and then the barrage was laid down. From where I was, as the barrage struck the sand, I could see it move up to the position like a curtain. Our troops in open formation followed up and the position was soon ours.

That evening prisoners began to arrive in large batches. As our cavalry and armoured cars had got round the back of the enemy's retreat it was cut off and his entire force and munitions captured. The most romantic thing in this business was the rescue of one of our own airmen and his restoration to his unit. This airman had gone out on an observation trip and never came back. He had been forced to come down in the enemy's country and taken prisoner. Along with a wireless section he had despatched by camel as a prisoner of war a day or so before the battle. This information, becoming known to the heads, meant armoured cars were sent out to try and over take the airman and his escort. After a great run they succeeded in the rescue.

My brigade, being detailed to clean up the battlefield, were at Khan Baghdad for some weeks. Khan Baghdad district was interesting. Here I found cave dwellers. In this part of Mespot there are lots of Whadis and large stone caves in which many Arabs live. The cave dwellers were poorly clad and had not the same hardy look of the average Arab down country.

At Khan Baghdad I met an office friend, Davie Bell. Davie had a narrow escape from a bursting shell, the top of which he was keeping as a souvenir. Davie was feeling and looking well but he died at Baghdad during the summer.

Temperance

I myself have no love for rum, and I don't think as a drink I would ever acquire a taste for it. Although I am practically teetotal, I never refused my rum ration. Much has been written, especially in the newspapers, for and against the issue of rum to soldiers but from experience I certainly plump for it. Rum is seldom issued unless necessary and I can assure you I found it beneficial. I remember when lying at Hit, we had no tents and very little bed clothing and as it came on very heavy rain for hours, I was bitterly cold, and we had every prospect of contracting some disease. An issue of rum was given and I took mine and got down to sleep and although everything was wet, and I lay in mud, I slept quite all right till morning and was none the worse.

In The East Time Is Of No Account

I first ran up against the truth of the proverb at Nasirych. I desired to have my watch repaired and after much trouble I discovered a likely place in the bazaar. It was only a small repair I wanted done to one of the hands, but the Arab watchmaker could not see his way to do it under three days. After much bargaining he at last promised to do it on the morrow. The morrow came but the repair was still undone, but in three days he succeeded. This is in spite of the fact that when you got to his place he was generally sitting smoking, a dreamy look in his eye as if he was thinking. This is the typical attitude of the Arab for his motto seems to be never to do today what you can do tomorrow.

In India it is the same. You can get plenty of promises but the actual performance is always put off as long as possible. I remember on reaching Kalyan junction that I went to the telegraph office to send off a wire. I stood at the counter quite a long time before a clerk came. When he did he slowly looked me up and down and asked, "Do you desire to send a telegram?" I replied in the affirmative. "Well," says he, "would you be so kind as to go away and come back in ten minutes as I am in a terrific business this morning."

To do business in India must be a slow job. Even at the post office to send a parcel requires a whole forenoon before you see it finally accepted.

The Call Of The East

In many books and places, I have come across the expression, "The Call of the East." Many stories have been written round this, but it is fraud. It should be called the call of laziness, for that explains the whole thing.

In India Mr Smith is sahib and Mrs Smith is memsahib. Taking into account financial standing you might get burrah sahib, which means big man – that is if he has plenty money. Take the average Briton in India. There he is with any number of servants, for labour is very cheap. The climate too is against very hard work, consequently he spends a large proportion of his time loafing. As it is a fine country, he can get his sport very cheap and have altogether a fine time besides being looked upon by the natives as someone of importance. The same Mr Smith if at home in England would sink to quite an ordinary average citizen, he would not be able to afford a tenth the number of servants, his sport would cost him ever so much dearer, and should he be in business he would require to work very much harder. Can we wonder then that after a taste of life in the East, and soon after return to England, the desire for the East comes on.

Mosul

Mosul stands on the west side of the Tigris and is bounded on the east by the river. The town is dusty, glaring, treeless and not picturesque. When viewed from a distance the outline of its walls are broken by numerous domes, universities and towers. Its buildings are mostly of Mosul marble and rock extensively quarried in the district and of varying colour from pure white to blueish grey. The city is partially surrounded by a rubble wall 15-20 feet high, about six feet broad at the bottom and three at the top. This was constructed at the beginning of last century as protection against Bedouin raids and is now out of repair.

The streets are narrow, undrained lanes winding between blank house walls. A few of the streets are paved with stones which make very slippery going. The houses are built of sundried bricks or Mosul marble sat in gypsum cement. Little wood is used in this construction. The larger houses are built round a courtyard into which the rooms and the hall open. They usually have under building or underground rooms for use in the hot weather. The number of houses have been estimated at 12000.

The climate is very trying during the hot weather from July to September, 120 degrees Fahrenheit and 95 at night. In the middle-ages Mosul was an important port of entry and manufacturing centre and was celebrated for its jewellery, arms and carpets as well as for cotton, silk and embroidered fabrics.

The word muslin is said to be delivered from the name of the town.

The population was estimated in 1904 as 400,000 to 500,000. Fully three quarters are Mohammedans and practically all of those Sunnis. The Mosul are a race of mixed origin, their language being Arabic. They have a bad reputation for turbulence, cruelty and viciousness. The drinking water at Mosul is very bad. The river when low is full of saltpetre and when high sulphur springs flow into it. There are plenty of wells but the water in them is very brackish.

Mosul is not a healthy place. It is built on a very bad site, which has at many times been under consideration of removal, but nothing yet has been done.

TB is prevalent but though there has been suspected cases it is clean of cholera. The opening of the Suez Canal and cheaper goods by machine manufacturer killed Mosul as a trading and manufacturing centre.

Babylon

By the courtesy of our officer Mr A.D.F. Thompson, a party of our brigade was granted weekend leave to visit the ruins of Babylon. We entrained at Baghdad Station and travelled to the ruins about 90 miles from Baghdad. The journey was done through the night, and we arrived at Babylon about 6 am on Sunday morning under the guidance of a Greek pastor, an official guide for the YMCA. It took us fully six hours to go over the ruins which were well worth the visit. The day was dull but nevertheless I secured many a good snapshot. The following are interesting facts concerning the ancient city.

Guide Note to Ruins of Babylon, authorities the Museum Guide Herodotus, Koldeway, Maspero, King, C Thompson.

Babylon. Greek name for ancient city called by its inhabitants Bab-ili, Gate of God. Lies five miles north of Hilla (90 miles south of Baghdad) on the Euphrates and consists of three principal mounds enclosed in a wall which has a circuit of about 11 miles. These mounds are known as Babil (north), Ksar (centre and east of the village of Knwairish), and Amran (south).

There was a certain amount of exploration by CJ Rich in 1811, Layard in 1850, Oppert from 1852-54 and Rassam from 1878-89. Work begun under direction of Dr Robert Koldeway on March 26th, 1899, and in spite of succeeding years of toil it is still unfinished.

Flint and other stone implements show that the site of Babylon was occupied in pre-historic times, that is before 4000 BC. The earliest historic ruins belong to the time of Khammurabiac, 2000 BC. These are the houses in the mounds of Merkes. These same mounds show houses of the periods of the Kassites (15th century BC), Assyrians (710-626 BC), Neo-Babylonians (625-538 BC) and later Babylon. However, the site owes much of its fame to Nebuchadnezzar the second (605-562 BC) who undertook the rebuilding of the centre city. It is the ruins of his work for the most part which the visitor to the ancient city sees.

The sketch map deals only with a portion of the left bank of Hilla. The river originally flowed from number one to Jumjumah village. Also note the sites of the city are included therein, including the position of Nibzo Palace on Kason Babil Mound, the Greek Theatre, Temples of Ishtar, Marduk's Tower of Babylon, and the ancient Bridge of Euphrates in the old channel. The Mound of Mirkes which contains the oldest ruins, remains.

It must be remembered Babylon has been used as a brick mine for centuries and portions above ground may have been removed to build Baghdad, Hillah, etc. The Turks added to their revenues by farming the rights to remove these bricks.

Starting from the Rest House and camp at *(1) Kirwairish Village and Rest House*, adjoining the recent residence of German Dr Koldeway, who carried out excavation research work prior to Greaburn 1914-18, follow the brack from one of the Kasr mounts to *(2)* which is the corner of the massive double wall, the remains of which are clearly distinguishable, its great breadth shown by the huge masses of brick work. The line of wall can be clearly traced, running east to minaret and south from the corner at *(2)*. Mounds to north and west show extension of quays towards riverbed.

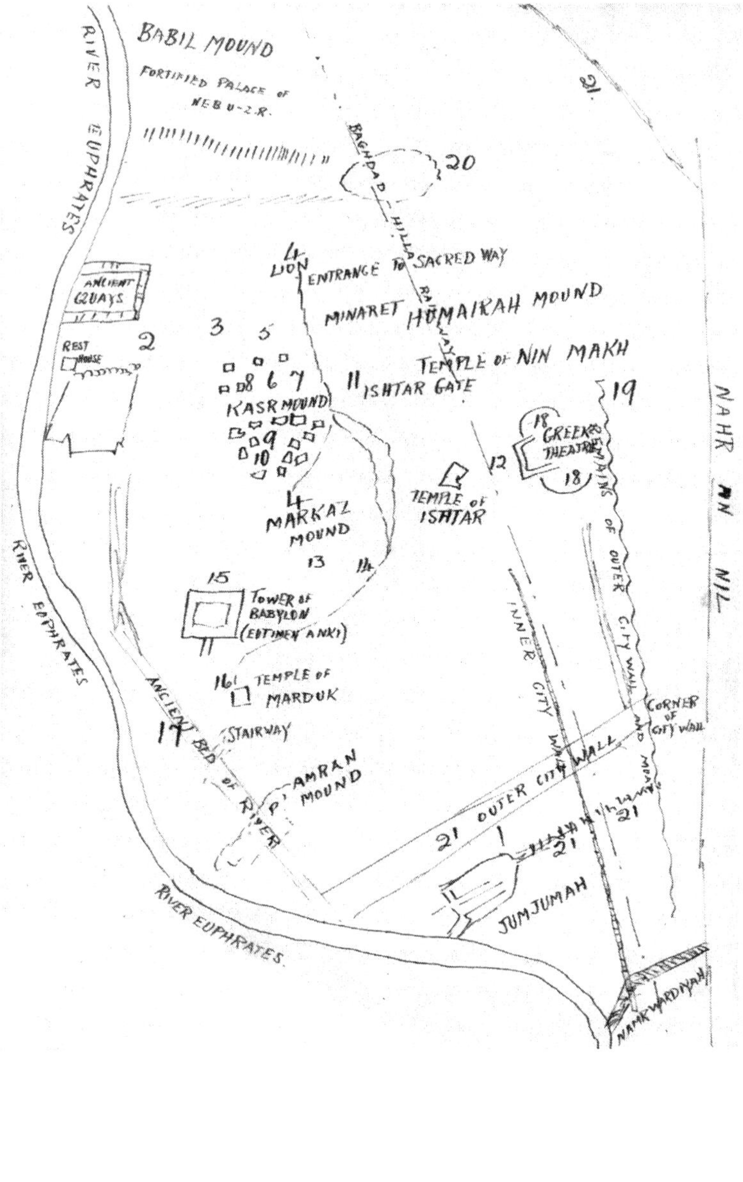
BABIL MOUND
FORTIFIED PALACE OF NEBU-Z-R.
RIVER EUPHRATES
BAGHDAD - HILLA RAILWAY
ANCIENT QUAYS
REST HOUSE
LION
ENTRANCE TO SACRED WAY
MINARET
HUMAIKAH MOUND
TEMPLE OF NIN MAKH
ISHTAR GATE
KASR MOUND
GREEK THEATRE
TEMPLE OF ISHTAR
MARKAZ MOUND
TOWER OF BABYLON
TEMPLE OF MARDUK
STAIRWAY
ANCIENT BED OF RIVER
AMRAN MOUND
OUTER CITY WALL
INNER CITY WALL
CORNER OF CITY WALL
JUMJUMAH
RIVER EUPHRATES
RIVER EUPHRATES
NAHR NIL

(3) Lion. This was probably one of several overlooking the great entrance to Citadel Palace and Sacred Way at *(4)*, supposed by some to represent Babylon conquering Egypt. The northern portion of Citadel Palace was more splendid than the south, its pavements of white and mottled sandstone, limestone and Basalt. The gigantic Basalt Bulls stood at the entrance near *(4)*. The Sacred Way (Processional Road) is distinguished at *(4)*, running south past minaret *(5)*. It is seen as a high level broad paved street running between two parallel walls through the magnificent Ishton Gate *(6)* and connecting the palace with the various temples whence the Gods were carried in procession. The brick pavements of the road still exist, covered with asphalt which formed a base for the flagstones. The centre is covered by limestone slabs more than a yard square, and the sides are laid with square blocks of red stone. On each slab was the inscription "I am Nebuchadnezzar King of Babylon; I paved the sacred way with blocks of stone for the procession of the Great Lord Marduck. Oh, Marduck Lord, grant long life." The walls were adorned with lions on each side in low relief, each over six feet long and spread out in enamel with yellow or red names and a blue background.

The Sacred Way led through the Ishtar gateway *(6)*, a double gateway with two separate gatehouses and with both outer and inner doors. This was because the inner-city wall comprised double walls, each with its own gate. The gates formed into a single structure by connecting walls, completing the enclosure of the gateway court. Side gates led between the walls. The beasts on the east wall are arranged as if advancing on anyone entering the Southern citadel – there were at least 575 of these creatures, those above ground level in white and yellow against a blue background. Much of the excavated gateway foundations were underground rooms for hot weather.

The Ishtar gateway leads to the open space *(7)* in front of the east side of the south citadel. Below and to right lies the roofless and many chambered vaulted building *(8)*. Cells arched over the originally several stories high hanging gardens. Onwards is the Temple of Nin Makh, Northern Goddess *(11)*, with its entrance facing north opposite one wing of Ishtar Gate. Many clay votive female figures were found here, made by woman who wanted children. The temple is oblong in shape with walls of sun-dried bricks. It has a central open court with many small rooms and a shrine room facing inwards in the centre of the south portion.

Scattered about the Palace of Nabopollasar are pieces of thick earthenware with blue glaze. These are fragments of coffins opened by brick robbers *(10)*. The throne room of Nibus is where the famous feast of Belshazzar as described in Daniel took place. Little more than the site can be identified *(14)*. From south of the Arman mound is seen Birs Nimrud, some seven miles distant. At *(15)* are the remains of a square tower, which some claim as the Biblical Tower of Babyl. It was known to Babylonians of all ages as Eutemen Anki, the house of the foundation stone of Heaven and Earth. At *(16)* is an excavated portion of the Temple of Marduk, most of which is still 70 feet below ground. Excavations have found a temple of great age, as shown by the sun dried bricks of very early times. A gateway centre *(17)* has been traced leading down to the river wall, where there are exposed several large earthenware urns in which the dead were buried in sitting position called "Pat Burials". This was a very ancient custom.

The Greek Theatre *(18)* was built in 325 BC. From the mound Humairah *(19)* is a good view of the general lie of the city, and around one and three quarters of a mile northwest the Babil mound (20) is visible.

Nibus built a fortified palace wall worth a visit. One inscription refers to it:

"On the brick wall towards the north my heart inspired me to build a palace for the protection of Babylon. I built there a Palace of Babylon, of brick and bitumen." Little scientific excavations have been done here so far.

Brief Historical Notes On Babylon

The ancient history of Babylon has been discovered from cuneiform writings, pictures and monuments. Cuneiform writing is a form of picture writing which started with actual pictures. Later these were abbreviated and written with a blunt reed on a wet clay. Moulds were made for Royal proclamations and copies taken from them, such as the bricks which name the King Nebuchadnezzar and state he built certain temples.

Books were written on these tablets, a large library of which was found at Mosul. An English soldier called Rawlinson discovered the alphabet. The writing spread from Sumer to Babylon and the oldest known slate dates before 4000 B.C. Sumer's towns were on lower Euphrates, north of the Chaldeans (where is found Abraham's reputed birthplace of Nasiriyah), Nipper, Larsa and Erech and others below Hilla. The people were of Turk stock with a highly developed culture and social system, and they excelled at mathematics and astronomy. They invented the uncial form of writing. Akkad – the second state – started somewhat later. The Bible states that Semites (from Arabia) under Nimrod the son of Cush built Babylon in the land of Shinar around 3800 BC.

Sumer and Akkad constantly fought each other, each in turn gaining supremacy, levelling towns, rebuilding on the top of ruins. This accounts for the different levels seen in the archaeology of the region, as well as the resulting mounds and traces of ashes in the ruins.

The sixth king Hammurabi enacted one of the oldest Babylonian codes of law. These show how advanced they were in and before the time that the Semites began to colonise the north and in form the separate kingdom of Assyria with its capital Ninerva, near Mosul.

Akkad and Sumer, both continually striving for supremacy, moved large armies to distant lands. Assyria now joined in and took its turn to conquer. Large armies marched to the Mediterranean, Egypt, Caucasus and Persia and returned with booty….

In 745 BC the Israelite tribes of Reuben and Gad from east of Jordan in Syria were carried into captivity to Assyria, where their descendants still remain. In 606 BC Medes from Persia conquered Assyria, which was then flourishing in its turn of ruling Babylon, which incidentally it had burned. This freed Akkad and enabled Nebopolassar to found a new Babylonian Empire. His son Nebuchadnezzer rebuilt the city and is responsible for much we see now. He captured Jerusalem and took many Jews captive, including Daniel. The tombs of Jewish prophets still exist there: Ezekiel's at Kifli, Daniel's at Mosul, and Ezra;s on the Tigris. Cyrus the Persian conquered Babylon in 538 BC.

From then onwards the city decayed and the centre of commerce moved to the Tigris, owing to its better navigation. Ctesiphon rose and fell into ruins and now finally has become the capital of this neighbourhood where great land and river routes meet.

The Tower Of Babel

The Birs Nimrod mound and the site of Borsippa is said by some to be the Tower of Babel. A cuneiform inscription shows that the present tower was built by Nebuchadnezzar (604-562 BC) and dedicated as the tower of the seven planets. The inscription states it was built on the site of a very ancient tower 450 feet high, the unfinished work of an unknown king of past ages. The older brickwork near the tower and that on Birs Nimrod hill is fused, evidently caused by great heat. Arabs say this is the result of lightning. These facts and the ancient legend appear to favour the claim that Birs Nimrud marks the site of the Tower of Babel.

The Tower of Babylon in Babylon City is considered by others to be a rival claimant. It is undoubtedly very ancient, but the debris is not such as one would expect on the site of a phenomenally large tower. It is important to realise the size and greatness of the city of Babylon. Herodotus, who actually saw it and who was accustomed to fine buildings in Greece, tells of its unsurpassed splendour and size, with houses three and four stories high, straight cut streets and traverses leading to the river, bitumen used as mortar, colossal walls, moats and fine decorations. The complete circuit of the city outer wall was 11 miles. This wall formed a rough quadrangle, divided diagonally by the river defences. Walls of burnt brick had eastern towers at intervals along the front double row of single buildings facing inwards with a roadway between broad enough for four horse chariots to turn, with a breadth of 100 feet.

It had a moat outside an inner wall, which protected city and temples. Babil mound built by Nebuchadnezzar protected against attack from North down Euphrates River and bridge. The river was spanned by a bridge connecting the two portions of the Town, roads led down to it each with a bronze gate. The piers of the bridge are still visible in the old bed.

Nebuchadnezzar's account of the building was found and translated. It reads as follows.

"I laid firm its foundation and raised it mountain high with bitumen and burnt brick. Mighty cedars I caused to be stretched out at length for its roofing. Door leaves of cedar overlaid with bronze I placed in its doorways. Silver, gold and precious stones, all that can be imagined of costliness, splendour, wealth and riches. All that was highly esteemed I heaped up within it. I stored up immense abundance of royal treasure therein."

OBSERVATIONS OF VISIT ON MARCH 1919

Scotch thistles and honeysuckle were in full bloom on the ruins. Coloured birds were seen too, all probably descendant from Nebuchadnezzar's time. The British are due praise for the excavations having performed most of the work. Money is now required to continue the research.

Did Nebuchadnezzar fear being poisoned, as he had a drinking well walled up high in his own chamber?

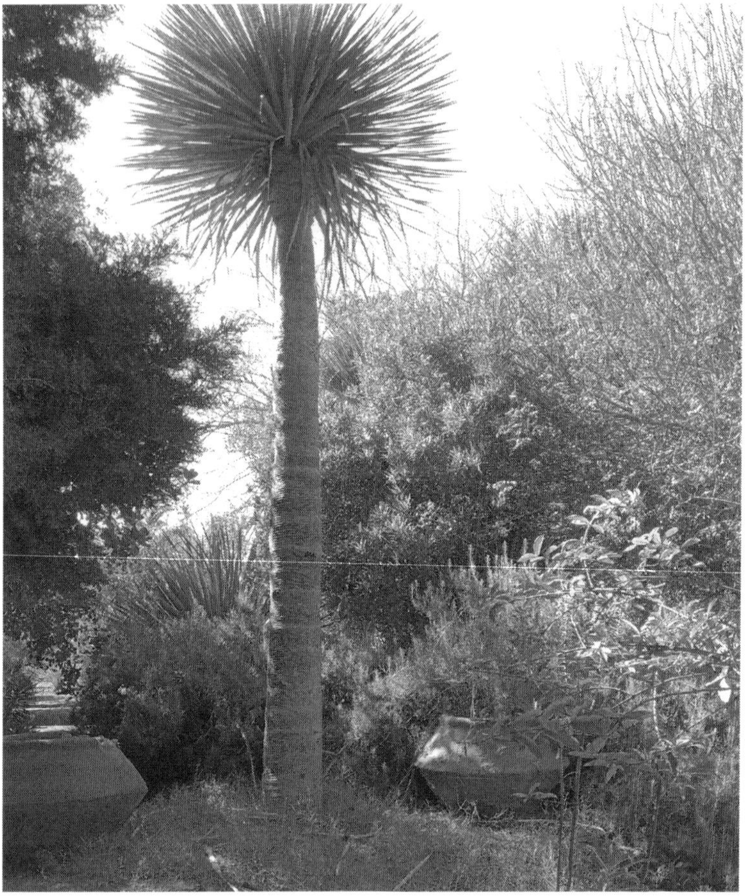

Code Of Khummurabi

The Code of Khummurabi was deciphered from extracts of cuneiform writing found on a large block of decorite stone. On the stone there is a picture of a god wearing a crown of four horns; two flames issue from his shoulders and the King of Khummurabi stands listening. The code consists of 202 articles of which the following extracts.

The first main heading deals with penalties to be imposed upon plaintiffs who attempt to influence defendants or witnesses by threats or corruption and decrees the punishment of death to a prevarication judge. The second enumerates the different kinds of theft with the responsibilities incurred under this heading defined by the town on whose territory the crime took place. The condition of the offices of the king, the police, and the collectors of taxes constitute the third section. Under a fourth heading are placed the numerous provisions for the cultivation of the land, leasing farms, irrigation, rights of pasturage, planting and the upkeep of orchards, the lending of money and the payment of debts between employers and employed. Provision for regulating the sale of liquors form a sixth section, certain articles of which impose capital punishment on the wine merchant who shall harbour conspirators and not give them up to the police.

The seventh section outlines methods of dealing with debtors. It provides for the case in which the creditor attempts to liquidate his debt by fraudulent seizure or take proceedings against a person against whom he can produce no legal proof of debt.

With article 127 begins a whole series of sections relating to the constitution of the family, to marriage, to the dowry of the woman, to the laws of inheritance. The ninth section opens with marriage. It decrees at the outset that for a marriage to be legal there must be a contract and it proceeds to enumerate the cause which may bring about a dissolution of the marriage.

The thirteenth section is entirely taken up with a scale of fines for blows and wounds. The lex talionis, eye-for-an-eye, approach is applied therein in all its severity. The scale of charges has unlooked for applications in the case of doctors, vets, surgeons and architects. They were liberally rewarded if successful, but if they injured their patients, or if the house built by the architect fell in resulting in a man or animal's death, the unfortunate cause of the disaster had to suffer mutilation, death or at least the penalty of paying a large sum of money.

From that point onward the code deals exclusively with commercial and industrial legislation, rights and obligations of shipowners, the hire and keep of oxen and other domestic animals, hiring of agricultural implements, day labourers, workmen and of boats, as well as the purchase and treatment of slaves. The discovery of this code has done more to enhance the memory of Khummurabi than if 20 triumphal inscriptions by him had been brought to light. It has ranked him with the greatest people of the human race.

Conclusion

On November 11th 1918, Germany formally surrendered and all the nations involved in World War One agreed to stop fighting while the terms of peace were negotiated.

On June 28th 1919, Germany, Britain, France, Italy and Russia all signed the Treaty of Versailles formally ending the war.

The conflicts of war devastate everyone, from civilians to soldiers. Many millions of people lost their lives, while many more went on living with both mental and physical trauma.

Royal Engineer Mr J.P McIntosh

Stanley McIntosh –
elder son of James P McIntosh

Born in Aberdeen, Mr Stanley McIntosh joined the Northeastern Fire Service at Aberdeen in 1939 and during his time in the National Fire Service was a Section Leader, Deputy Commandant with No. 5 FF, an instructor at the Scottish Fire Service Training School, Training Officer, then Station Officer with the same fire force. He married and had a daughter. Stanley McIntosh had been Deputy Firemaster for six years before joining the Lanarkshire brigade around 1951. He was Assistant Firemaster in Lanarkshire for eight years. In 1961 he was awarded an M.B.E for distinguished service.

There is a commemorative plaque at Motherwell Fire Station bearing the names of Assistant Firemaster Stanley McIntosh and Station Officer Joseph Calderwood who died as a result of fire/explosion at Colvilles Limited, Mossend Works, Bellshill on Monday 7th January 1963.

After a dedication ceremony by the Rev Peter Houston, Mr James Irvine, chairman of Strathclyde Regional Council's police and fire committee, unveiled the memorial plaque, paying tribute to those fine officers and the whole of the fire service. Stanley McIntosh's funeral was held on 11th January 1963.

There is also a firefighter memorial trust book of remembrance online.

A public inquiry was held at Airdrie Sheriff Court, where the jury returned a formal verdict that deaths in each case was due to multiple burns.

Stanley McIntosh MBE